Enjoy!!

from Adeline

9/27/94

CAT
HOROSCOPES

FOR EACH OF YOUR CAT'S NINE LIVES

CAT HOROSCOPES

FOR EACH OF YOUR CAT'S NINE LIVES

GENIA WENNERSTROM

HARRY N. ABRAMS, INC.
PUBLISHERS
NEW YORK

INTRODUCTION

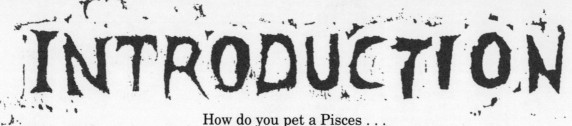

How do you pet a Pisces . . .
Cuddle a Capricorn . . .
Love a Libra . . .
Stroke a Sagittarius . . .
Gentrify a Gemini . . .
Lead a Leo . . .
Tame a Taurus . . .
Appease an Aries . . .
Captivate a Cancerian . . .
Accommodate an Aquarian . . .
Value a Virgo . . .
Snuggle a Scorpio?

The answers lie in the stars. If all of our lives are shaped by the signs
under which we are born, then cats have horoscopes too.

If destiny brought you and your cat together, then CAT HOROSCOPES
can enhance that relationship by astrologically defining compatibility
for your single- or multi-cat household.

A pedigreed cat comes with papers to prove its birth date,
but how can you tell with a stray? Very easily.
Your stray's new life started when it arrived on your doorstep.
Its new birth sign is derived from that day.

But remember, if your pet's personality
doesn't match its birth sign,
you can always choose another,
more compatible, sign
from among your
cat's nine lives.

ARIES
rules the head. Aries like to bump heads in greeting and love being petted, especially around the ears.
MARCH 21 – APRIL 19

TAURUS
rules the throat. The home of Taurus is filled with purring. They love "pets" on the throat.
APRIL 20 – MAY 20

GEMINI
rules the arms and hands. Gemini will extend a helping paw – usually onto your plate.
MAY 21 – JUNE 20

CANCER
rules the chest and stomach. They are fond of tummy rubs. They also gobble their food.
JUNE 21 – JULY 22

LEO
rules the heart. Proud, brave Leo the lion-hearted is a lap cat during the day and sleeps snuggled by your side at night.
JULY 23 – AUGUST 22

VIRGO
rules the colon. A Virgo keeps a clean litter box, but try to keep Virgo from giving a public display of cleanliness.
AUGUST 23 – SEPTEMBER 22

LIBRA
rules the kidneys. When bending over, watch out for Libra's "kidney punch" while jumping unexpectedly on your back.
SEPTEMBER 23 – OCTOBER 22

SCORPIO
rules the reproductive organs of this highly sensual sign. Spay, spay, spay…and alter.
OCTOBER 23 – NOVEMBER 21

SAGITTARIUS
rules the hips. When chasing their tails, Sags are swivel-hipped.
NOVEMBER 22 – DECEMBER 21

CAPRICORN
rules the knees. But *they* love rubbing against *your* knees.
DECEMBER 22 – JANUARY 19

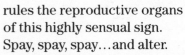
AQUARIUS
rules ankles. Yours, for nipping and for running in between.
JANUARY 20 – FEBRUARY 18

PISCES
rules the feet. Pisceans don't pussyfoot around. They jump, usually on you, in bed, at dawn.
FEBRUARY 19 – MARCH 20

ARIES

THE RAM   PLANET / MARS   MARCH 21 – APRIL 19

You can always tell Aries by the nips in their ears and the scars on their noses.
Like their astrological symbol, the Ram, Aries lead with their heads.

Inquisitive Aries, persistent Aries, first-anywhere Aries are not scaredy cats,
as their nips and scars show.

The Marco Polos of the cat world, Aries are natural leaders,
always the first to explore new situations.

And why not? That is the destiny of their birth, for Aries is the first sign
of the zodiac and symbolizes beginnings.

That "fast-forward" blur of fur racing through the house
for no apparent reason is probably an Aries being influenced
by its ruling planet, Mars, which gives Aries raw, unbridled energy.

And, like the ram, Aries communicates by bumping its head against yours.

"Good morning." Bump, bump.
"I'm hungry." Bump, bump.
"Oh, were you away?" Bump, bump.
"Good night." Bump, bump.

At dawn, if you hear the lid of the cat food bin opening and closing
by itself — bump, bump — it's just that help-yourself, first-to-try Aries
has discovered how to open the lid by using its head — literally.

If you see a jaunty cat coming down the road with a perfectly
formed spider web crisscrossing its face, that's a curious Aries.

If you hear a tree meowing, look up. Aries is at the top,
where Aries belongs, up high . . . first . . . number one!

Compatible with:

GEMINI AQUARIUS LEO SAGITTARIUS LIBRA

TAURUS

THE BULL   PLANET / VENUS   APRIL 20 – MAY 20

Who is that mashing down the marigolds, snuggled close to Mother Earth,
lying in a sunbeam? Taurus. Down-to-earth, unpretentious Taurus.

Taureans roll and revel in the grit and dirt of driveways or country roads,
coming home with mica-flecked fur and shaking sediment
from earth's top layer onto your rug.

Taurus, the physically strongest sign of the zodiac, is also gentle and kind.
In fact, Taurus will stand away from a bowl of milk
if a very aggressive head pushes in to drink from it first.

This is not a sign of timidity. On the contrary, self-assured Taurus feels
no need to prove strength. Taurus knows that one swipe of the paw will
show any doubting Thomas the power of the gentle giant.

For Taurus is an anomaly, mixing the strength of the Bull
with the sweetness of its ruling planet, Venus.

Since Taurus also rules the neck and
throat, the home of a Taurean is filled
with purring. In fact, if you are
looking for your Taurus at home,
look with your ears.
You will hear Taureans
before you see them,
their large frames squeezed
into something small and cozy,
their loud purring interspersed with
an occasional snort or snore,
sleeping the sleep of the innocent
. . . or the indolent.

Compatible with:

SCORPIO VIRGO CAPRICORN PISCES CANCER

GEMINI

THE TWINS   PLANET / MERCURY   MAY 21 – JUNE 20

Pet, pet, pet. Purr, purr, purr.

You and your bundle of fur are having a moment together,
when *suddenly* — whop!

For no apparent reason, your darling claws you,
then immediately settles down, paws folded under,
and smiles directly in your face.

Purr, purr, purr, once again.

How can such a sweet face have such sharp claws?

No offense intended.

You are simply dealing with the duality of a Gemini,
ruled by the planet Mercury, hence its mercurial nature.
Gemini also rules the hands and arms, hence the "whop."

Impulsive Gemini. Affectionate Gemini, and intelligent.
Twice as smart as anyone else. In fact, Geminis are brilliant.

Who opens the bedroom door by hanging on the knob and
giving it a twist? Gemini.

Who knows how to tell time so that you don't need an
alarm clock in the morning? Gemini.

Who turns on the answering machine by stepping on
the right buttons? Gemini.

And who always answers when you talk? Gemini.

For Geminis love to communicate, love to talk . . .
or remain silent. Planet Mercury, remember?

If you live with a Gemini, then lucky, lucky you.
For the price of one . . . you get two.

Compatible with:

ARIES AQUARIUS LEO SAGITTARIUS LIBRA

CANCER

THE CRAB   PLANET / MOON   JUNE 21 – JULY 22

Home is where the heart is.
And that is where you will always find your Cancerian.

In fact, if not sleeping on your head at night, a Cancerian will probably be
snuggled next to your heart . . . and snoring. For, despite their
baby faces, Cancerians wheeze and snore loudly
when sleeping — and Moon children love to sleep.

Cancerians like to ask questions, usually in the form of a long-drawn-out
meow that can end up in a yawn. But they get their point across, because
they will keep asking until you answer . . . and you always do.

Despite the Crab appellation in their astrological sign, Cancerians are
anything but. They are soft, loving, and gentle but tend to be apprehensive.

The only crablike link to their sign is that Cancerians often get their
claws caught in screens, carpets, or your good clothes. And, as
with crabs' claws, you have to extricate them carefully.

But Cancerians never complain and are very patient; in fact, they will always wait until you are almost finished eating before "pawing" your plate.

A Cancerian will follow you throughout the house as if magnetized to your body.

If your telephone bills are very high, it is probably because you have a Cancerian who jumps onto your lap at the sound of your dialing the telephone, then settles down and purrs.

What cat lover can disturb that scenario?

Compatible with:

SCORPIO, PISCES, TAURUS, VIRGO, CAPRICORN,

LEO

THE LION   STAR / SUN   JULY 23 – AUGUST 22

Leo is different. Leo has to be noticed. Leo is always on stage.

Ruled by the Sun, Leo shines.

Leo is warm, affectionate, loving, adorable . . . when Leo wants to be.
Otherwise, Leo can be skittish, selfish, and loud.

Leo needs no one — but wants to be noticed by everyone.

Leo doesn't like to share . . . a dish, an empty box, a room. Leo is a star!
Leo wants its own dish, its own empty box, its own room.

A Leo will lovingly lick your eyelids in the morning to wake you up,
then "paw" you (claws out) from its perch as you walk by.

Leos assume outrageous positions awake or asleep.
Who knows when someone with a camera will come by?

Leos make good single pets. They like the
limelight, centerstage. They want your love
all for themselves and will return that love in
great abundance (especially when you are
engrossed in reading or work).

A Leo will never disappoint you or never bore you
with its ever-changing theatrical persona.

Leo cats are probably the only animals you can clap
your hands at loudly and not have them cower.
In fact, Leo will probably give you an encore.

Compatible with:

SAGITTARIUS ARIES GEMINI LIBRA AQUARIUS

VIRGO

THE VIRGIN   PLANET / MERCURY   AUGUST 23 – SEPTEMBER 22

You can always tell Virgos by the white gloves they wear — or at least they
act as if they're wearing white gloves — and by the sweet scent of their heads.

Graceful Virgo. Charming Virgo. Modest, quiet, and clean Virgo.
Neat — even prissy — Virgo "tidies up" the leftovers from everyone's plates.

Fastidious Virgo digs a hole almost through the litter box,
to make certain that everything is ecologically covered.

Although Virgos are basically loners, they will even lick clean other cats
in close proximity (sometimes against the grain). Virgos are usually the ones
who will lick your fingers, especially after you've put on hand lotion.

Perfectionist Virgos manicure and pedicure their paws
until their nails are thigh-puncturing sharp.

Ruled by the winged feet of Mercury, female Virgos walk gently,
as if on high heels. Male Virgos' paws seem to glide above the ground.

Virgos are always on the move. They always find new comfy spots,
which other cats then appropriate.

But Virgos are never distressed. They have an air of tranquility about them.
Look into Virgo's surprisingly clear, deep, gentle eyes, and you will instantly relax.

Now, wouldn't that make *you* want to purr?

Compatible with:

CAPRICORN PISCES TAURUS CANCER SCORPIO

LIBRA

THE SCALES   PLANET / VENUS   SEPTEMBER 23 – OCTOBER 22

If you want a real live cuddly teddy bear to sleep nestled
in your arms at night, choose a Libra cat.

Libras' sweet and loving natures are shaped by their ruling planet, Venus.

Companionably loving and cozy at night.
Companionably alert and aware during the day.
Libra's balanced personality comes from its astrological symbol, the Scales.

Highly intelligent, Libra will share your interests by sitting on the paper you are
reading at the moment, or "writing" with the pen you are using,
or "helping" you with your food.

Libras practice strong eye contact. You may not even be familiar
with your Libra's back, for they always face you, looking directly at you
and speaking volumes with their large, expressive eyes.

Venus gives the Libra cat a very soft, whispery voice, but
balances it with perhaps the most amplified purr in the zodiac.

Librans love music and they love flowers.

Hearing their favorite TV theme song usually brings them running
to the set to plop down on a convenient lap and listen contentedly.

And their love of flowers? Librans sit on them, too!

Compatible with:

GEMINI AQUARIUS LEO SAGITTARIUS ARIES

SCORPIO

THE SCORPION   PLANET / PLUTO   OCTOBER 23 – NOVEMBER 21

Scorpios are wonderful! Forget their negative symbol of
the stinging Scorpion and their netherworld ruling planet, Pluto.

Scorpios are loving and tender. Scorpios are devoted and faithful.

Not for anything are the brightest stars of the zodiac found in the
constellation Scorpio. If our lives are shaped by the stars under which we
were born, then Scorpios are probably the most intensely brilliant,
sparkling personalities on Earth.

The astrological sign of Scorpio also rules reproduction,
and some Scorpios take that sign seriously.

But they do tend toward jealousy.

If you see someone glowering and counting
the "pets" you are giving the *other* cat in your house,
the glowering one with the green eyes can only be Scorpio.

But loyal, a loyal friend.

Scorpio is the one who would walk a thousand miles
to find you if you moved away, because Scorpio
wants to stay with you, through thick and thin.

Alchemists of old believed that, when the Sun
was in the constellation of Scorpio,
iron could then be easily turned into gold.

Even in ancient times,
Scorpios were thought of as pure gold.

Compatible with:

TAURUS PISCES CAPRICORN VIRGO CANCER

SAGITTARIUS

THE ARCHER   PLANET / JUPITER   NOVEMBER 22 – DECEMBER 21

Sagittarius rules the world . . . or so Sagittarius feels.

Your home is Sagittarius' domain.

In fact, Sagittarians think the world ends at the boundaries of their property and that the world is all theirs. Sagittarians rule it all.

But not with guile or cunning — ever.
Sagittarius' face reflects only straightforward honesty
and an innate self-esteem.

Sagittarius is Top Cat. Has anyone said otherwise?
Sagittarius would be surprised.

Agile, inquisitive, friendly . . . Sagittarius bears no malice.
"Chasing the other cats? What? I was only playing!"

At night, under the influence of their astrological symbol, the Archer,
Sagittarians aim straight for your bed, pawing the blankets, hunting
for your legs, then flinging themselves down, settled for the night.
No circling around three times for them. Sagittarians are decisive.

Sagittarians are the perfect weight and warmth on your legs
because they keep themselves trim. They exercise every day,
even if only chasing their own tails.

A Sagittarius is the one you always see at the front door,
waiting for you to come home.

A Sagittarius has many friends, because a Sagittarius is loyal and true.

Everyone loves gregarious Sagittarius.

Compatible with:

GEMINI   LIBRA   ARIES   LEO AQUARIUS

CAPRICORN

THE GOAT   PLANET / SATURN   DECEMBER 22 – JANUARY 19

Should you consider that kitten?
The quiet one, a bit wistful-looking, frail, with a snuffly nose.
Yes! Take *that* particular kitten home!

That frail kitten is probably a Capricorn, and you will
be rewarded with many, many, many years of happiness,
for Capricorn is the zodiacal sign for long life.

The tenacious Goat, butting its head, pressing on through the years,
spinning those rings of Saturn around its peers
as Capricorn goes on and on and on.

Think of it! A constant, loyal, affectionate companion
for years and years to come.

And healthy. No vet bills with Capricorn.
The sickly kitten grows into a robust adult.

Dependable, steady. You will never hear that sound of rejection —"thump, thump" — as when other cats jump off your lap or bed. Capricorn, the stubborn goat, reliable and steadfast, will always stay by your side.

In fact, if you have a golden-ager, who remembers when shredded newspaper was used in the litter box, who still can't get used to the new litter (it gets stuck between the toes), perhaps, as a treat, for old-time's sake, on your Capricorn's birthday, order a newspaper to be delivered — shredded. For Auld Lang Syne.

Compatible with:

TAURUS VIRGO CANCER PISCES SCORPIO

AQUARIUS

THE WATER BEARER   PLANET / URANUS   JANUARY 20 – FEBRUARY 18

Whose furry, perky head is tilted to one side, drinking water directly from the faucet? Must be an inventive Aquarius.

Not only because the Water Bearer is its symbol, but because Aquarius is also the sign of genius.

Over seventy percent of those listed in the Hall of Fame have Aquarius in their sign or their ascendants.

But then, if you already have an Aquarian living with you, you are not surprised.

Your Aquarius probably already knows how to pop-pop-pop the food dish with its paw when hungry, or to just help itself from the table if you're too busy.

Your Aquarius can probably change TV channels by simply shifting its position on the cable box.

Your Aquarius probably knows how to play your bedroom door like a bongo drum . . . at dawn.

Genius . . . but a very friendly genius.

An Aquarian is the one that other cats snuggle up to. An Aquarian is a loyal friend.

Good-natured Aquarius, lively and intelligent.

Astrologically, the sign of Aquarius brings with it good fortune.

While the rest of the world awaits the Age of Aquarius, you may already have the good fortune of living it now, with your own famous Aquarian.

Compatible with:

GEMINI LEO SAGITTARIUS ARIES LIBRA

PISCES

THE FISH   PLANET / NEPTUNE   FEBRUARY 19 – MARCH 20

Like the Fish in their zodiacal sign, Pisceans move
with liquid smoothness, gliding in and out
around your ankles, back and forth, silently,
on paws that seem never to touch the ground,
so flowing is their gait.

Gentle Pisces, shy Pisces, sensitive Pisces.

And emotional Pisces. Ruled by the planet Neptune,
Pisces purrs tears of joy from half-closed eyes
when petted, or stroked, or brushed.

Count on compassionate Pisces to always
be there in your "down" moments.
Pisces will unblinkingly look you in the eye and,
without ever shifting paws, listen, listen, listen.

Better than a shrink session is a long conversation
with your sympathetic Pisces.

Perhaps for that reason, big-hearted Pisceans tend to have big ears. The better to
hear you with. But even though Pisceans have an uncanny memory, they also are
very silent. They practice a mock meow — an opening and closing of the mouth with
no sound. They never tell all they know. Your deepest secrets are safe with a Pisces.

Like the sonar sounds of the sea, reverberating in Neptune's deep, Pisceans are
attuned to the vibrations of their own surroundings. Psychic Pisceans always know
when you are returning home. They will get up from a sound sleep and go to the front
door before you even put a key in the lock.

Pisces knows . . . but Pisces never tells!

Compatible with:

SCORPIO VIRGO CAPRICORN TAURUS CANCER

Library of Congress Cataloging-in-Publication Data

Wennerstrom, Genia
Cat horoscopes: for each of your cat's nine lives / by Genia Wennerstrom
p. cm.
ISBN 0-8109-3185-0
1. Astrology and pets.   2. Cats–Miscellanea.   3. Astrology and pets–Humor.   4. Cats–Humor.   I. Title.
BF1728.3.C43   1992
133.5'86368–dc20   92–7835
CIP

Published in 1992 by Harry N. Abrams, Incorporated, New York
A Times Mirror Company

Printed and bound in the United States

SWEET DREAMS